BOOKS BY JAMES MERRILL

Poetry

THE INNER ROOM   1988
LATE SETTINGS   1985
FROM THE FIRST NINE: POEMS 1946–1976   1982
THE CHANGING LIGHT AT SANDOVER   1982
SCRIPTS FOR THE PAGEANT   1980
MIRABELL: BOOKS OF NUMBER   1978
DIVINE COMEDIES   1976
BRAVING THE ELEMENTS   1972
THE FIRE SCREEN   1969
NIGHTS AND DAYS   1966
WATER STREET   1962
THE COUNTRY OF A THOUSAND YEARS OF PEACE   1959
(REVISED EDITION 1970)
FIRST POEMS   1951

Fiction

THE (DIBLOS) NOTEBOOK   1965
THE SERAGLIO   1957, 1987

Essays

RECITATIVE   1986

The Inner Room

The Inner Room

Poems by

James Merrill

Alfred A. Knopf   *New York*

1988

THIS IS A BORZOI BOOK
PUBLISHED BY ALFRED A. KNOPF, INC.

Library of Congress Cataloging-in-Publication Data

Merrill, James Ingram.
    The inner room.
    I. Title.
PS3525.E664515   1988   811'.54   88-45265
ISBN 0-394-47248-3
ISBN 0-679-72049-9 (pbk.)

Some poems in this work were originally published in the following
publications:
COLUMBIA, THE DENVER QUARTERLY, ERATO, FOUR QUARTERS, GRAND STREET,
MICHIGAN QUARTERLY REVIEW, THE NEW YORK REVIEW OF BOOKS, POETS &
WRITERS, RARITAN, THE SOUTHERN REVIEW, TEMENOS, VANITY FAIR, and
VERSE.

"Grace" was originally published in THE ANTIOCH REVIEW, Volume 45,
Number 1, Winter 1987.

"Processional" was originally published in THE ATLANTIC MONTHLY,
November, 1982.

"Arabian Night," "David's Watercolor," "Hindu Illumination," "Icecap,"
"Losing the Marbles," and "Serenade" were originally published in
THE NEW YORKER.

"A Room at the Heart of Things" was originally published in
THE PARIS REVIEW.

"Anagram," "A Bit of Blue Tile on the Beach," and "Voltaire: A Statue of
Christ" were originally published in PLOUGHSHARES.

"Morning Glory" was originally published in SHENANDOAH.

"The Fifteenth Summer" was originally published in SOUTHWEST REVIEW.

"Walks in Rome" was originally published in THE YALE REVIEW.

The play "The Image Maker" was privately printed by Sea Cliff Press, New
York in 1986. It was first performed on May 27, 1986, by Mary Bomba and
Peter Hooten under the joint auspices of the Los Angeles Theater Company
and the UCLA Center for the Performing Arts.

Manufactured in the United States of America
First Edition

For Peter Hooten

CONTENTS

I

I I

I I I

Contents

I V

V

I

LITTLE FALLACY

Chamber of blossom, not a petal spilled,
Yesterday's Japanese cherry
—You and I charmed inside the glow—
By evening had borne fruit:

A whole day in Beirut
—According to the radio,
The first since January—
With no one killed.

DECLARATION DAY

Shiners dance counter to the tide.
The dragon kite, all wagging tail,
   Hangs fire in a fair gale.
No trace of knowledge called inside,

Where after daybreak, as a gust
Of radiance unsealed its doom,
   An entire fresco'd gloom
Crumbled gratefully to dust.

The pool. Drowned leaves beset the drain:
Crown-deep how long in pale cement,
   Poor laureate?—till blent
With flash and ripple from your brain

Up swim two figures, surfacing.
Crosslight of blue flares, hazel flares.
   Noon bells. The garden chairs
Simply keel over in a ring.

A rose. The two as one. To wit,
Petals encompassed and exact,
This heart that opens to contract,
And, beating time, grows out of it.

The bower. Shadow of a space
   For picture-taking. Each
Foiling the sun in turn, they teach
His brightness to the smitten face.

And now the moment. The house tried
   To warn them. It's of hard
White pine stained dark as a lifeguard,
With lips and brows of zinc oxide.

Down even the dim hall they burn.
    A door just floats ajar.
The stillness trembles like a star.
A wish. Come true? Here's where to learn.

Unnoticed, evening falls. Night falls.
    In one another's glow
Foreshadowed attributes take slow
Possession of the old, primed walls.

MORNING GLORY

for Howard Moss

1

The *bud* a foreskin? More so as it wilts—
The vine of any afternoon
Drooping with once radiant antennae,
Now purplish, drained, the rite of passage done,
That generation's at-a-blow adults
Going obediently to seed.

As if a plant could disobey!
—In whose encyclicals ego alone
Is sacrilege. Why, even among the blue
Tuareg of the Atlas foothills a certain few
Will have remained, like you and me,
True to the miracle, or its memory:

The single day, at six or seven,
When each was little but a wide-ribbed heaven
Tuned wholly to the cosmic one
Of pulsing depths, blue deepest overhead,
And where, though busy Eros visited,
All we knew, all we lived for, was the Sun.

2

That talent scout
Meanwhile kept untold millions in view.
Intending everyone (as you know who
Posited deadpan) to be famous
Precisely for his hour in the sun,
The roving eye alit, over and out,

Cast through taut silk the shadowplay
Of lives-to-be. Yet how one given day
Allowed for Byzantine intrigue
With many a new twist

6

As the ascending tangle of spotlights
Became itself protagonist—

Art nouveau poster: August, matinée
Idol whose averted
Gaze the atavistic Greeks
Lament on dancefloors, in their Sulka-shirted
Nightmare of lucre: *The sun
Hasn't seen me for weeks!*

3
From afternoon shade
Where the others, sated and bruised, have called it quits,
A virgin frill emits
Wrong signals. Able neither, caught in vines,
To open and espouse
The world nor (consequently) to fade,

What have we here? Well, well!
Eye-shadow on an old maid? A clear case,
Dear colleague, of that syndrome—Down's—
In which the fontanel
Forecloses early on its full
Quota of intelligence. *Not all there,*

Yet touching, even gay,
It strikes a note sadly malapropos
—Or so, shaking our gray
Heads, we agree.
Its very dying is suspect,
Flaunted. A last shred of indecency.

4
Crete, 1975. Edward, one's friend,
Alcoholic but a gentleman—
Stabbed on the stair in his elegant shell of a house

Morning Glory

Twenty-six times. The "other American,"
Pierce, blue-eyed novelist, nastily bright,
Owing him money—out of town that night.

The killer was *his* friend:
Village blade whose mutant tendencies
Village manners might have held in check.
Instead, the daily session
Up on Pierce's cantilevered deck
Was teaching Spiro to Release Aggression.

Sober for once (affirmed the weeping cook
At the taverna where the foreigners ate)
Edward had gone home early. There he found
Spiro hunting for the IOUs.
Fierce ultra-violet shone to saturate
All three. A form gone limp. The midnight news.

5
Every day the line of bloom gets higher,
And now the topmost flares
Go off, sky-bright in bright sky. There's
No last-ditch rescue for—or from—our own
Natures, who so aspire
To the unknown.

Any charring from those bursts of fire?
Open just one
Tiny bronze-purple thurible: briquettes!
Black as coal next year, they'll catch, they'll climb,
Repeating their tribe's miniature
Resurrection myth, where seed is savior.

For like the Sun, behavior that begets
Calls for a camera obscura
To distance, or domesticate, it in.
It's the unknown,

Here in these stanzas, in your lover's eyes—
The radiant pinhole shadows fertilize.

6
But, Howard, at eighteen,
When first in bud, half open to the world,
What prompted us? And flowers—what were they?
The "thought" wired home on Mother's Day.
Who'd have conceived
A god's arrival by such idling green

Machines as ours, all veinwork, exhibition;
A Poem's giving up its throne
For Life, the commoner,
At her messy vanity—disposable issues
And cleansing screams, her latest instrument
To curl the hair . . .

Now more and more we furl asleep
Waking into the next blue "lighted tent"
Of song and story
Nicely made up, like her. For her!
The world at last our own to reinvent,
This or that bit gets titled "Morning Glory."

7
Violet, the sinister of blue . . .
Frost killed the vine. That morning it
Swung man-high
Where four winds crossed. I also felt the stab.
Our local Color Lab
Came up with images. My favorite—

(Remember the roof-garden, its lamppost
Crowned with a rusted fixture
First holding gaslight, now just sky?

9

Morning Glory

Year-round ring for clouds to tumble in
Or tedium to blow
Great bubbles through—)

Anyhow, my favorite
Has "green hearts" and pristine cornets
Twining until the iron aureole
Drew to its vacancy for once a face
So human, so in focus, word
Went flashing, pole to pole:

CONNECTICUT MAN FOUND IN STATE OF GRACE

SERENADE

Here's your letter the old portable
Pecked out so passionately as to crack
The larynx. I too dream of "times
We'll share." Across the river: MUTUAL LIFE.

Flush of a skyline. Owning up to past
Decorum, present insatiety,
Let corporate proceedings one by one
Be abstracted to mauve onionskin,

Lit stories rippling upside down in thought
Be stilled alike of drift and personnel,
Then, only then, the lyric I-lessness
At nightfall banked upon renew

Today's unfolder. Whose lips part. Heard now
In his original setting—voice and reeds—
As music for a god, your page
Asks to be held so that the lamp shines through

And stars appear instead of periods.

WATERSPOUT

Where foam-white openwork
Rumples over slate,
Flash of a fork, the first
Wild syllables in flight,
The massive misty forces
Here to be faced are not
Of wind or water quite
So much as thought uptwisted
Helplessly by thought,
A fullblown argument
Sucked racing through whose veins
Whitebait and jellyfish
Repeat the lacy helices
Threaded into the stem
Of a Murano—wait:
Spirits intoxicate
The drinker, not the glass;
Yet *goblets*—three of them—
Weave up to be counted
Like drunks in the stormlight.
Self-dramatizing scene
That cries and reels and clouds . . .
From somewhere above clouds,
Above thunder and levin
And the herring gull's high scream
(At which one glass may seem
To shatter), from this heaven
Slaked by the spinal fluid,
A bright-eyed reveller
Looks down on cloth outspread,
Strewn silver, fruits de mer,
The lighthouse salt-cellar—
A world exhausted, drained
But, like his word, unbroken;
Looks down and keeps his head.

DAVID'S WATERCOLOR

Dusk. The old cloaked shepherd of terracotta
standing guard, front center. A weak, unshaded
bulb you worked by throws, from offstage, his shadow
onto the blue wall.

Shutter flung wide. Glow from my downstairs desk-lamp
shows how close we are to our neighbor. Further
up the dark street, luminous rifts distinguish
household from household,

flat from flat, each climbing the common hill, each
lit its own way. Wires like birdflight swoop in
insulated pairs—they've been mates so long now—
gracefully skyward.

Restless late last night, I switched on your Key West
guestroom light. There, dead to the world, my young love
lay. The scene hung over his head, its message
sweet, unemphatic:

Fifteen years this hillside was home. Let someone
else's eye be grazing those Greek horizons.
High in space, sunlit (the one source we still trust)
glimmers a new moon.

ARABIAN NIGHT

Features unseen embers and tongs once worried
bright as brass, cool, trim, of a depth to light his
way at least who, trusting mirages, finds in
them the oasis,

what went wrong? You there in the mirror, did our
freshest page get sent to the Hall of Cobwebs?
Or had Rime's Emir all along been merely
after your body?

No reply. Then ("there" of course, also) insight's
dazzle snaps at gloom, like a wick when first lit.
Look! on one quick heartstring glissando, stranger
kindles to father

thirty years a shade, yet whose traits (plus others
not so staring—loyalty, cynicism,
neophyte's pure heart in erotic mufti
straight out of Baghdad)

solve the lifelong riddle: a face no longer
sought in dreams but worn as my own. Aladdin
rubs his lamp—youth? age?—and the rival two beam
forth in one likeness.

TWO FROM FLORIDA

I   *Green Cove Springs*

Aqua concrete has girdled this inveterate
Uppouring from Earth's heart, at 3000 gallons per minute.
A sign recounts the excellent things in it,
Among them calcium, iron, magnesium sulfate.

Thus fortified, it proceeds to fill the municipal
Plunge, free to the public from May through November.
(Limbs in my father's day flashed, as he liked to remember,
From a now-defunct, excitingly "private" pool.)

With almost professional quickness and tact it takes
The imprint of some dozen random figures, then
—Goodbye to that small floating world of women and men,
Their upside-down stucco hotel rechristened ANTIQUES—

Having arrived at a lucid, babbling sufficiency
White sand and green grass pave, between banks of grass
Yellowed by frost's dispassionate coup de grâce,
It joins the St. Johns River to the Sea.

2   *The Dresden Doll*

Mis' Annie looks just like a Dresden doll,
People would say about my mother's mother
All her life, particularly after
She came back from Europe *with* a Dresden doll.

That must have been around 1930?
The doll, of porcelain like her little chair,
Had panniered skirts and piled-up, powdered hair,
But sat, as women did by 1930,

Legs crossed, with a pert smile—the platitudes
Of rotogravure—bewildering unless
From someone I ought to have known, in fancy dress.
Would we all harden into attitudes?

Painted more pertly each decade, my grandmother
Crossed her short-skirted legs and sipped her toddy,
Chatting about everything and everybody,
Even what it was to be poor, and a young mother,

In Jacksonville at the beginning of the century.
People, as it were, kept brightly dusting some dull
Irrevocability from the living doll,
Dead nonetheless this quarter century,

While the other perches on my bureau, here to stay
Little as I now want it, under its glass bell,
A smiling figure—punishment as well—
For what I simply can no longer say.

THE FIFTEENTH SUMMER

Scrambling with a book
The hundred-or-so feet
Up the Australian pine
To a slung-rope seat—
The nerve it took!

Small wonder, often as not
He never read a line,
Flaubert or Howard Fast,
Just pondered earth and ocean,
The odd car's crawling dot:

Why were we here?
To flow. To bear. To be.
Over the view his tree
In slow, slow motion
Held sway, the pointer of a scale so vast,

Alive and variable, so inlaid
As well with sticky, pungent gold,
That many a year
Would pass before it told
Those mornings what they weighed.

A ROOM AT THE HEART OF THINGS

Two rooms, rather, one flight up, half seen
Through the gilt palm-fronds of rue Messaline.

Sparse furnishings: work table, lamp, two chairs,
Double bed, water closet, fourteen stairs;

Six windows, breathing spaces in the plot,
Between its couplings, to enjoy or not.

A poster—Carnival's white eyeless faces.
The ceiling fan. The floor the actor paces

From room to room, getting by heart the lines
Of boards washed ruddier as day declines,

Of fate upon the palm slapped to his brow,
Of verse the instant they are written (*now*)—

His shadow anyman's, chalk walls a trite
Clown-camouflage all comers penetrate.

*

The role he studies—a Young Man in love—
Calls upon self and the eclipse thereof

By second nature. Evenings, dazed from sun,
Earth buries her worn faces one by one

Deeper in fleecy quilts, dusk atmospheres,
Then high-up quivering Hesperus appears.

Just so, the actor, deep in middle age,
Assumes a youth till now unknown. On stage

Within a stanza to be somehow first
Turned inside out and only then rehearsed,

It's this one's pen he seizes, and lamplit
Page he corrects. Soon he may read from it

Tonight's draft of the curtain line (Act II):
"Light of my life, I've made a play for you!"

★

Reduce, said Malraux, to the minimum
In every man the actor. Brave bonhomme,

Coming from him—! Beret and cigarette,
The worldwide field-reporter style was set

By how he posed, key witness to his time,
Questions of moment, face a paradigm.

We plain folk who believed what we were told
Had seen our crops burnt and our wives grown old

In one same night. Malraux alone took note,
As all who could read, would. Neat, was it not?

Life gave the palm—much the way God once did—
For "living biographically" amid

Famines, uprisings, blood baths, hand to heart,
Saved by a weakness for performance art.

★

Those ivory towers were bric-a-brac. One flight
Of wooden steps, one slapdash coat of white,

Sets the room hovering like a UFO
At treetop level. Spellbound by the glow,

Moth hallucinates and cat outstares
The glamor of dimensions never theirs.

A Room At the Heart of Things

Its tenant treads a measure, lights a joint,
Drawing perspective to the vanishing point

Inside his head. Here vows endure beyond
Earshot of lovers who dissolved their bond;

Whitewash keeps faith with tenements of dew
Already atomized to midnight blue;

And Gravity's mask floats—at Phase XV
Oblivion-bright—above the stolen scene.

*

Actor and lover contemplate the act
So-called of darkness: touch that wrestles tact,

Bedsprings whose babble drowns the hearing, sight
That lids itself, gone underground. Torchlight

Gliding down narrow, redly glimmering veins,
Cell by cell the celebrant attains

A chamber where arcane translucences
Of god-as-mortal bring him to his knees.

Words, words. Yet these and others (to be "tarred"
And "set alight" crosswise by "Nero's guard")

Choreograph the passage from complex
Clairvoyance to some ultimate blind x,

Raw luster, rendering its human guise.
The lover shuts, the actor lifts his eyes.

*

By twos at moonset, palm trees, up from seeds
Big as a child's heart, whisper their asides—

Glittery, fanlike, alternating, slow
Pointers in the art of how to grow!

They have not relished being strewn before
Earth-shaking figures, Christ or Emperor.

Profoundly unideological
Wells of live shadow, they are no less tall

Pillars of strength when—every twenty-six
Millenia, say—their namesake the Phoenix

Comes home to die. (Stylite and columnist
Foretell the early kindling of that nest

—Whence this rustle, this expectant stir?)
The actor robed as priest or birdcatcher

★

Steps forth. The room at heart is small, he smiles,
But to the point. Innumerable aisles

Converge upon its theater-in-the-round's
Revolving choirs and footlit stamping grounds.

Only far out, where the circumference
Grazes the void, does act approach nonsense

And sense itself—seats cramped, sightlines askew—
Matter not a speck. Out there the *You*

And *I*, diffracted by the moiré grid
Have yet to meet (or waffled when they did!),

But here, made room for, bare hypothesis
—Through swordplay or soliloquy or kiss

Emitting speed-of-light particulars—
Proves itself in the bright way of stars.

11

The Image Maker

A PLAY IN ONE ACT

CHARACTERS

The SANTERO *(Manuel)*
His MOTHER
JUANITA, *his niece*
FRANCISCO ⎫
MIGUEL ⎬ *santos*
BARBARA ⎭

*The santos are puppets and may if necessary be oper-
ated, and their lines spoken, by the actors themselves
from backstage. As the* MOTHER *never appears, her
lines may be spoken by* JUANITA *in the voice of an old
woman.*

The Santero's workshop in a Caribbean village. Two finished san-
tos stand in a recess behind him. To his right, a door open onto the
street. To his left, the curtained entrance to an inner room. A cot, a
chair, a tiny stove. Three or four logs stacked in a corner, for future
carving. A caged bird hangs cooing in the morning light. A calen-
dar on the wall says clearly: MAY.

SANTERO   I am the Santéro Manuel.
              It's I who make the images
              For the entire community.
              My works are in the mountain villages
              And in the little boats far out at sea.
              Wherever people work or dwell
              Some figure that I've made
              Keeps them and theirs
              Safe and sound and unafraid.
              The santo works, too, to dispel
              The dark within them, hears their prayers,
              Then maybe says a word on high
              To the old Image Maker in the sky.

              I'm getting famous! Down at the Hotel,
              An English tourist wants to buy
              Anything I make. But I say, why
              Go to such trouble if it's just to sell?

              It's never easy! First I choose
              My wood and age it. Laurel, oak,
              Rosy cedar or the capa wood
              That, kindled, gives out fragrant smoke,
              Proving its nature sweet and good.
              And then my different dyes and glues,
              Metallic powder, colored clay,
              Red, blue and ocher, black and white—
              All these must be at hand.
              Before each job I fast a day
              Until my head is light,
              Until my hand is true.
              Certain other things, you understand,
              I am required to do

At moonrise on the final night,
But may not speak of that to anyone.

At last the figure is begun.
And never mind how well
I know my saint, I'm in for a surprise
Or two before I'm done—
A crafty smile, a new, hard-pressed
Look in the eyes . . .
I clean my tools, and while the last coat dries,
Lie down and try to rest.
It's never easy.

MOTHER   *(from the inner room)*   Manuel!

SANTERO   Mamá?

MOTHER   Have I drunk my sweetened milk today?

SANTERO   Yes, Mamá, not an hour ago.

MOTHER   What about Pepé? Have you fed Pepé?

SANTERO   Of course, Mamá. *(Explains)* Our dove, Pepé.
Of course I fed him. Don't I love him, too?

MOTHER   And what's to eat at noon?

SANTERO   Cornbread. Enough bean soup left in the pot
At least for one.

MOTHER   A mother's blessing on you, faithful son!
Make sure it's good and hot.

SANTERO   *(resuming)*   Now if you wish
I'll show you two I finished just last week.
Francisco, there, knows how to speak
With birds and wolves and fish.
Therefore he is the go-between
Who keeps alive good will
Among all creatures, and the hunter clean
In spirit for the kill.
And over here's Miguel

Who cast the Devil down
From Heaven's citadel.
He's a great angel. See his crown?
See his gold scales? In them he weighs
The light of all our days.

JUANITA   *(in the doorway with a bundle)*   Uncle . . . ?

SANTERO   Juanita, child, come in. What have we here?
Why it's a friend from years ago,
Saint Barbara. Her dress I made
Out of the wide red sash my mother wore
In the first Independence Day parade.
Your mother's her namesake.
What's wrong? Did something break?
Architecture and artillery
Are Barbara's double specialty.
When thunder dances on the roof rough-shod,
She's better than a lightning rod.
You've brought her back, though.

JUANITA   She's always taken care of us, but . . . Well,
First the milk turned sour, you know?
And then the sugar box got filled with salt.
Concha pretends it was my fault.
And then Antonio—
He told me that he'd be away
On business until Saturday,
But Concha saw him last night late
Downtown with Rosa. Now I'm full of hate!
Then Concha—my own sister—gave a sneer
And said, "Go ask our Uncle Manuel
For a true-love spell
And get your boy friend back, Juanita dear—
Or try!"
I hate her too! I want to die!

SANTERO   Nothing else?

JUANITA   Well, the mule's lame.

27

I don't believe the Saint's to blame,
And told our Grandma so,
But she looked in the mirror and said, "Go.
There's always something, to our shame,
Wrong with the world. So take her to Manuel."

SANTERO *(standing the figure between the other two)*
Leave her with me. She looks worn out.

JUANITA Then Grandma grumbled—she's lame, too, with gout—
And said, "Look for bad news beneath the paint
Even of the household saint."
Uncle, what did she mean?

SANTERO Why, just that God has many faces,
And different names in different places.
Come,
I'll walk you home.

JUANITA And my love spell?

SANTERO Brown cheeks, green eyes,
Love is its own spell, don't you realize?

They go out. The santos come to life.

BARBARA This god with faces—has he powers
Like ours?

MIGUEL He made the Earth, the Stars and Sun.

BARBARA How should we know?

MIGUEL He made the Man.

BARBARA The man says so.
He also says in tones
That chill
My bones,
"God's will be done."

MIGUEL The man made us.

BARBARA   You see now? Without further fuss
          Let's have some fun—
          Let's do man's will!

Blackout. Then moonlight. A cloth drapes the birdcage. The San-
tero lies sleeping. In this scene Barbara speaks with the Mother's
voice.

BARBARA   Bad son, bad son—
          Where's my bad, lazy son?

SANTERO   Me lazy? Bad? When all I do
          Is cook your meals and make your bed?

BARBARA   And leave me in it! Ha! Confess it's true
          You wish me ill, you want me dead!

SANTERO   Mamá, you're dreaming! Or am I?

BARBARA   You never married—why?
          Am I supposed to die
          Without grandchildren? What a life!

SANTERO   My work, Mamá. That's *my* whole life. Admit
          I'd have no time for child or wife.
          But don't I love you? Don't I care for you?

BARBARA   Care for me? Care for *me!*
          Ha! If you cared one bit
          You'd throw these dolls out no one pays you for,
          And get work at the factory.

SANTERO   Mamá, I beg you, I implore—

BARBARA   Be still! I'll have a fit!
          If you were half the son that you pretend,
          Gold would come out of you as soon as shit,
          And with the money in my purse
          I'd take a first-class train to the world's end!

SANTERO   What have I done?

BARBARA   I'll tell you what, halfwit—

29

You've made me ill!
A mother's curse
Upon you! Ay, ay, ay!
Run, wake the pharmacist! I'll die
Without a stomach pill!

Fully awake by now, the Santero sits up, slips on his sandals, and without thinking to look in the other room, rushes into the street. The light changes to include all three santos and the birdcage.

BARBARA   This god—is he a master
           Black or white?

MIGUEL   He made the bat, the rooster,
          The black she-goat.

BARBARA   He made the priest.

MIGUEL   The priest tells wrong from right.

BARBARA   Or only sees by full-moon light
          Which beast
          To kill.
          He draws the blade across the throat—
          A floor of blood!

MIGUEL   Our sawdust vitals drink their fill.

BARBARA   Why shouldn't God?
          Brother, do his will!

The third santo, Francisco, throws back his head and utters several loud, hawk-like cries. Under its cloth the dove calls, flutters in panic, falls silent with a small thud.

BARBARA   Bravo! Now, Brother, stealer of fire, your turn.
          Something to burn?

MIGUEL   First be it understood:
          No man shapes *me*
          From a block of wood,

Paints *my* face with white clay,
Dresses *my* mind in dimity.
I am the Light of Day,
I entered the forbidden Tree,
And every other tree since then.
I am the generator.
By reason's lamp or fever's flickering ray
I make the Image Maker.
Whatever god is magnified by men,
I, I stare through their glass until
He does my will!

The calendar on the wall bursts into flame. Consternation.

BARBARA   Oh, no! A book, a chair—
              Never the calendar!

MIGUEL   There go our holy days
              Up in a flash!

FRANCISCO   Caw! Caw!

BARBARA   The month of May's
              Already ash!

MIGUEL   What was to come, ablaze!

BARBARA   Keep it away from my skirt!

MIGUEL   Don't let it melt my scales!

BARBARA   So bright—my eyes hurt!

MIGUEL   So hot—my heart fails!
              Save us before we expire!

ALL   Save us! Caw! Caw! Help! Fire!

They break off as the Santero returns. He tears down the calendar and stamps out the fire. Calmer now, recalling his mother, takes the pills and a cup of water to her door, but does not enter.

The Image Maker

SANTERO   Sleeping . . . She slept right through . . .

Only now thinks to check the birdcage.

> Pepé! Ah so.
> This is your work, Changó.

Behind him, Barbara twitches to attention. The Santero lays the dead bird at her feet, and assembles within reach: necklaces, spices, a candle, a cigar, etc. A small drum or bell he will strike at intervals.

> Changó, no more! Drop your disguise,
> Or pick on someone your own size.
> Work through the Popes, the Presidents,
> Figures of influence.
> Work through a poor santero if you must,
> But spare these simple clods
> Of paint and dust.
> Don't tempt them to distress—
> As man does Earth and Air and Sea—
> The houses they were made to bless,
> Or, when they've drawn like poultices
> A thousand lifelike fears and fantasies,
> To act like gods.
> Changó, away! Take your artillery
> To Addis Ababa or Zanzibar.
> Away! Our dove Pepé has died.
> Drink up its blood. Be satisfied.
> Changó, away! I've lit
> The strong cigar
> You love. Inhale the smoke. Vanish like it!

Begins to chant.

> CHANGO MANI COTE CHANGO MANI COTE
> OLLE MASA CHANGO OLLE MASA CHANGO
> ARA BARI COTE CHANGO ARA BARI COTE

ADA MANI COTE ADA MANI COTE
ARA BASONI COTE CHANGO MANI COTE
OYE CHANGO ARA BASONI COTE
ARA BARI COTE CHANGO ARA BARI COTE
CHANGO MANI COTE CHANGO MANI COTE
OYE CHANGO ARA BASONI COTE
ARA BARI COTE OYE CHANGO

*Throughout the above, which may be freely varied or prolonged,
the figures—Barbara in particular—struggle. On the final convul-
sion there comes a feeble pop and flash in the air above their heads.
Five beats. A roll of distant thunder. The santos stand in a row,
chastened. Day is breaking.*

*The Santero tidies up. Out goes the dead bird, on goes milk to
warm. He arranges his tools, takes Barbara from the recess, and,
after a reassured glance into the next room, sets to work.*

Forgive me, Lord, if I presume
To show You how to do Your work.
From Your high, starry room
You overlook the murk—

Interrupting his prayer to talk to himself.

Look at this bad scar,
See how the color cracks and chips.
No wonder fumes eclipse
The morning star.

—The murk that clogs the mind
And eats away its godlike face.
Take us in hand, as I do these.
Lord, change mankind!—

A wash of alcohol,
A touch of healing gum . . .
There now. A final crumb
Of white on the eyeball . . .

33

         —Take us in hand, as I do these.
         Repair, freshen, efface,
         So that unswerving grace
         Flows through Your images.—

         We'll hide that angry red
         Under a cloak of blue.
         Now, Barbara, maybe you
         Will keep your head?

         No more explosions, understand?
         —And, Lord, make us unlearn
         The skills that wound us, blind and burn.
         Take us in hand.

MOTHER   *(from within)* Manuel!

SANTERO   Mamá?

MOTHER   Have I drunk my milk today?

SANTERO   Not yet, Mamá. Good morning! Are you well?

MOTHER   How can I tell?
        Always the same. Forgetful, fat and old.
        Ready for breakfast anyway.

SANTERO   Milk's warming now. You wouldn't want it cold.

MOTHER   Good son. And have you fed Pepé?

SANTERO   Mother, our poor Pepé . . .

MOTHER   And what's to eat at noon, eh? Something nice?

SANTERO   Well, if the Englishman at the Hotel
        Keeps his word, meets my price
        And buys Francisco and Miguel—
        Chicken and beans and rice?

Takes the milk in to her. Francisco and Miguel exchange a look, and shrug. Returning, the Santero removes and begins to wrap them.

MOTHER   *(cackling)*   Chicken and beans and rice . . .

SANTERO   If I can pay,
Chicken and beans and rice.

JUANITA   *(at the door)*   Uncle, good day!

SANTERO   Well, well. Come in.
Do I see a change?

JUANITA   Don't tease me! It's the true-love spell.
Grandma knew exactly what to do.
You hollow out a gourd
And put inside
Your lover's name—Antonio—
With something that he's given you—
A flower I'd kept and dried.
Then five drops of perfume,
Five peppercorns and . . .

SANTERO   *(resigned)*   Cinnamon.

JUANITA   Pepper and cinnamon, a rooster's comb—
They sell them at the corner, cured—
Then light a candle in the room
And say a prayer to . . .

SANTERO   To all the saints in Rome.

JUANITA   Saint *Clara*. As if you didn't know!
And then Antonio's sister came today,
Just now. He *was* away.
Faced with the truth, Concha admitted she
Was only teasing me!
The ferry-boat arrives at ten o'clock.
I want to be there at the dock.
Goodbye!

SANTERO   You've time. First take this home.

Hands her the figure of Barbara.

JUANITA   Oh, Uncle! Look, she's changed her dress!
She's beautiful—like an actress.
Aren't her eyes bigger? That's not her old smile.
Will she be good now?

SANTERO   Yes.
Well, for a while.
You be good, too, child—or I'll have you hexed!

Juanita runs off, laughing. Ready to leave with his two bundles, the Santero pauses, puts them down. He selects an uncarved log and sets it upright in the empty recess. Studies it a long moment. Sighs.

What next? What next?

III

THE PARNASSIANS

Theirs was a language within ours, a loge
Hidden by bee-stitched hangings from the herd.
The mere exchanged glance between word and word
Took easily the place, the privilege
Of utterance. Here therefore all was tact.
Pairs at first blush ill-matched, like *turd* and *monstrance,*
Tracing their cousinage through consonants,
Communed, ecstatic, through the long entr'acte.

Without our common meanings, though, that world
Would have slid headlong to apocalypse.
We'd built the Opera, changed the scenery, trod
Grapes for the bubbling flutes mild fingers twirled;
As footmen, by no eyelid's twitch betrayed
Our scorn and sound investment of their tips.

MENU

Dawn. Mist for the grill. As our visual purple
Unfurls to usher in another day,
Highnesses of Appearance are discovered
Touring—with us—the Smokies. Dubious figures,
Like all their subjects. That bearded and bandanna'd
Kid outside the laundromat could be
Nature's nobleman, a local dirtbag,
Or one disguised as the other. Smell this coffee.
Its molecules, as you bend your head to them,
Outwhiz the edge of space. Exciting, but
Why the incognito, and will it never
Be seen through? Is my dread of the electorate
Justified or fatally naive?
What relation has the mother cat
To (a) her litter, (b) the barrio
Women who corner her, and (c)
The TV coverage of their meal? To what
Degree was Gandhi neither fish nor fowl,
The War of the Roses an innocuous masque,
The brook our supper table? (Ragged white
Cloud-cloth, blue plates of calm, courses in swift
Succession chattering on to pebble mints . . .)
Mental sleights and tints and taints untold,
Only perhaps reflected in a dewdrop
Or viewed from Venus do they concentrate
Into a single beam, though it too flickers.
Satiety meanwhile, or something not
Unlike it deep in things, calls for the check.
That's why the cabin floor was strewn with petals,
And the brook, backsliding helplessly all night,
Clutched its bed for dear life, knuckles white.

FOR A BESTIARY

1 *Carp*

"Bread on the waters." Would
Such literary crusts
Do for their thrash of lusts?
Half fiction was the food

Too many times already
Snapped up in expectation.
Simply to keep the ashen-
Filmy, flame-gilt eddy

Banked in its grate of reeds—
An underwater fire,
How lit?—might prove desire
Itself the fast that feeds.

Yet, alchemy beyond
Fresh lapses into gold
Having made blood run cold
Throughout the pivot-pond,

Come winter, seal them in,
Unplug the glittery nerves,
Lidding those red preserves
With rime's white paraffin

On which a skater writes
(Ah, loop and curlicue
Of letters we once knew)
Here sleep the appetites.

2   *Spell*

Three times a triple strand
Of quietly ticking wire
Is wound about what were
Acres of wonderland

Cropped bare now. One prize ox
Gazes in mute appeal
At grass beyond the pale:
Terrestrial paradox,

Which drawn-to-by-degrees,
Weird, rough-and-tumble veldt
Of voltage, jolt on jolt,
He'll sooner starve than graze.

The vignette touches you?
Be my guest, let him out!
—And yourself in, no doubt,
For a shock or two.

3   *Monday Morning*

Hot sun on Duval Street.
Bicycling very slowly
I see, by all that's holy,
An acute blur of fleet

Parrot-green plumage coast
Onto the bus-stop bench:
Less bird, after all, than mensch
"Free as a bird"—its ghost

Face cocked. Now Daddy Kaiser
Of Angelo's Cut 'n Comb
Waddles forth, spry gnome
Waving his atomizer,

Diamonding with spray
One instant hedonist!
Pure whim? Fair-weather tryst?
Already a block away,

I keep risking collision
(In each year's crazier traffic)
To fix that unseraphic
Duo within my vision.

HINDU ILLUMINATION

T loping down the stairs at Mellifont.
That end-of-March, half-mad, half-mocking
Duel with O. NR's
Forearms, who taught me pinochle at ten.
E's glow of pure seduction as it stole
Throughout a nature presently
To be reviled by it. (Reviled? Revealed.)
P's helpless laughter. H's body heat . . .
Remembering all these and more, I smile.

Likewise an artist made his elephant
Entirely of interlocking
Animal and human avatars:
Antelope, archer, lion, duck, each then
Reborn as portion of the whole
Proverbial creature—wisdom, memory—
Shown dancing on a crimson field.
Now, reaching for you in pitch dark, to meet
The mahout's gaze, upon me all this while.

GINGER BEEF

Soon to attain its famous afterglow,
The mountain drinks late sun. Below and early,
Shown to the terrace, we two pause, as always
Silenced by green fields, cottonwoods, the pond,
The two (same?) swans, their nest
Empty at this season. Close beyond's
The low clay house my friend—twelve years ago?—
Rented, only to move. And move again,
A painter's eye in quest
Of the ideal arrangement. While this scene
Didn't quite serve his purposes, no less
Radiant, forgiving and serene,
It takes him in as always, head to foot
—Where a new six-month puppy plays the fool.

They'll have found other tenants for that house—
Two rooms—in which I came to see him first:
House where, cold evenings, he and I, the dog,
Gazed, all three, into the blazing log;
Where he and I drained the last drop of red
Before he and the dog went off to bed;
From which, excited mornings, we'd all pile
Into the truck—we two in the front seat,
The dog behind us—and drive mile on mile,
Vast backdrop rippling heat . . .
When the run ended, did the cast forget
Those properties, that unstruck, sunstruck set?

Creak, offstage, of a screen door
—Our hosts? Instead, impossibly, appears
(As when "for charity" a legend acts
Despite old age, arthritis, cataracts,
The role that made her famous) who
But . . . Ouspenskaya in a dog suit? Or
Who herself! The very dog, those years
Imprinted by her master raptly crooning

Ginger Beef

"Who are you? *Who* are *you?*"
(Mix of coyote, shepherd, malamute)
Till Who at last was all she'd answer to.
Slowly now she limps the length of terrace,
Lashes gone white beneath the widow's peak,
To kiss—no prompting now or ever—
His palm, then mine: *Yes, here's*
That friend of His I grew
To tolerate, let stroke me, soul and senses
Fixed on the roadside store
He'd presently, if I kept faith, once more
Emerge from. As He did, at first. But then . . .

But then life's thrifty. Every day a bit
Gets put aside, the why and where of it
A puzzle, till the nest egg hatches—wings
Whistling through us as the pieces knit.

Isn't the right place everywhere, and found
By everyone? Some, though, turn round and round—
Ever about to settle, never quite
Able to do so—on the faithful ground.

Fear of belonging, or inflicting harm?
Friends gestured from their niches. "Pure dull charm"
Kept at arm's length—no. Make the story short.
He gave the dog to these two, for their farm.

Of course it hurt. His reasons were austere
As rainlight, as the two-or-three-per-year
Landscapes he showed us. But with what wry phrase
Of mine shall I give *him* away? For here

Our hosts come. Bright-eyed lookalikes, hair shot
With silver, smiles of puckered apricot,
Their manners—all our manners—past reproach.
I wonder how we bear it. Who does not.

For her, it's more . . . more like tonight's pièce
De resistance.—Lift from the crock, let stand;
Then chill, trim, slice, and recompose
Within its essence, clarified topaz
(Afterwards, find a moment, thank the cook)
Of a deliciousness—
                    She comes to sniff,
But is too dignified to take,
The surreptitious morsel from my hand.

Fields green still, heights their celebrated red
Well after sunset, past the panes
Flashes the puppy yapping—in Who's stead?
With passion she recalls? Yes, and disdains:
Eyes nowhere, slumping down on stone
In mute, in mortal weariness, alone.

Nambé, 1981

EIGHT BITS

I   LASER MAJESTY

Light show at the Planetarium.
Schlock music. Seven colors put through drum
Majorette paces. "We saw God tonight,"
Breathes Wendy. Yes, and He was chewing gum.

2   IF U CN RD THS

u cn gt a gd jb w hi pa!
So thinks a sign in the subway.
Think twice when letters disappear
Into Commodity's black hole—
No turning back from that career.
This counterspell may save your soul.

3   *VOLTAIRE:* A STATUE OF CHRIST IN JESUIT ATTIRE

Admire these monks' excessive art
And industry who've dressed you, dear
Lord, in their very robes for fear
Lest someone take you to his heart.

4   ANAGRAM/ANAGRAMME

Here *Pasolini* lies, decorum's foil,
Writhing in PAIN and crumbling into SOIL.

Ci-gît *Pasolini,* après de longs effrois,
Son corps devenant PAIN, ses cris devenus LOIS.

48

5 LIPSTICK, 1935

At Aunt Pearl's kiss the pointed head
Extruded glistening pale red
From the jet sheath where it was housed
Looked like our Labrador, aroused.

6 SNAKE PIT

Uplands. The dead of winter. Yet you've seen
Mist rising from an April ring of green
(We're massed beneath, all moistly interlaced)
Whose self-engendered garden in the waste
Shows Eden as it were "by natural light,"
And Baptist ranchers where to dynamite.

7 TO AN ACTOR ON LOCATION FOR A FILM
   IN WHICH HE GETS KILLED

Who live a life so charmed, time and again
The spear goes through you but you feel no pain,
Who rise amused, even as Earth receives
A battered image and the housewife grieves,
Go forth to die, Adonis. Then let's dine
Your first night back in town. My place at nine?

8 A BIT OF BLUE TILE ON THE BEACH

Fragments like this, my Sunshine, fall
When you flash from your shower stall.

DEAD CENTER

Upon reflection, as I dip my pen
Tonight, forth ripple messages in code.
In Now's black waters burn the stars of Then.

Seen from the embankment, marble men
Sleep upside down, bat-wise, the sleep bestowed
Upon reflection. As I dip my pen

Thinking how others, deeper into Zen,
Blew on immediacy until it glowed,
In Now's black waters burn the stars of Then.

Or else I'm back at Grandmother's. I'm ten,
Dust hides my parents' roadster from the road
Which dips—*into* reflection, with my pen.

Breath after breath, harsh O's of oxygen—
Never deciphered, what do they forebode?
In Now's black waters burn the stars. Ah then

Leap, Memory, supreme equestrienne,
Through hoops of fire, circuits you overload!
Beyond reflection, as I dip my pen
In Now's black waters, burn the stars of Then.

I V

Prose of Departure

for Donald Richie

Imagining it.

Paul phones to say goodbye. He's back in New York two days early, but we are tied to our trip—departure this evening—and he, for his part, doesn't ask us over. (Can a single week have changed him? Surely not.) Our dear one sounded strong, unconcerned, above all glad to have left the Clinic. Famous and vast and complex as an ocean liner, it catered chiefly to elderly couples from the Plains. Whether both were ill, or just the husband or the wife, they'd chosen not to be separated. They slept (as did Paul) at the nearby hotel, then spent their waking hours together in lounges, the magazine unread, or strolling hand in hand the gleaming, scentless corridors from one text—one test, rather—to the next. Paul, though, was by himself, was perhaps not even "sailing." Waiting to hear over his own system the stern voice calling *Visitors ashore!* he would have begun to feel that, aside from the far too young and noncommittal crew, bona-fide passengers only were expected to circulate there, all in the same boat, their common dread kept under wraps, yet each of them visibly

> at sea. Yes, yes, these
> old folks grown unpresuming,
> almost Japanese,
>
> had embarked too soon
> —Bon voyage! Write!—upon their
> final honeymoon.

Arrival in Tokyo.

Our section of town is Roppongi, where thirty years ago I dined in W's gloomy wooden farmhouse. The lanes and gardens of his neighborhood have given way to glitzy skyscrapers like this hotel—all crystal and brass, a piano and life-size ceramic Saint Bernard in the carpeted lobby. It is late when the revolving door whisks us forth, later yet when our two lengthening shadows leave the noodle shop to wander before bed through the Aoyama cemetery. Mishima is buried down one of its paths bordered by cherry trees in full, amazing bloom. Underneath, sitting on the ground—no, on outspread plastic or paper, shoes left in pairs alongside these instant "rooms"—a few ghostly parties are still eating and drinking, lit by small flames. One group has a transistor, another makes its own music, clapping hands and singing. Their lantern faces glow in the half-dark's black-beamed, blossom-tented

> dusk within the night.
> The high street lamp through snowy
> branches burns moon-bright.

Donald's Neighborhood.

NARROW streets, lined with pots: wistaria, clematis, bamboo. (Can that be syringa—with *red* blossoms?) Shrines begin. A shopkeeper says good day. Three flights up in the one ugly building for blocks around, Donald welcomes us to his bit of our planet. Two midget rooms, utilitarian alcoves, no trace of clutter. What he has is what you see, and includes the resolve to get rid of things already absorbed. Books, records. His lovers he keeps, but as friends—friends take up no space. He now paints at night. Some canvases big as get-well cards bedeck a wall. Before we leave he will give the nicest of these to Peter.

What are we seeing? Homages to Gris, Cornell, Hokusai, Maxfield Parrish. Three masters of compression and one of maple syrup. Without their example, where mightn't his own work have gone? (Would he have painted at all?) As for his album of lovers, without the archetypal Uncle Kenny to seek throughout the world, who mightn't he have loved? And what if he hadn't settled in Japan forty years ago? Living here has skimmed from his features the self-pity, cynicism and greed which sour his Doppelgänger in that all too imaginable jolly corner of Ohio.

Later—stopping first at a bookstore to buy what they have of Donald's in stock—we proceed to the projection room, where at our instigation we are to be shown six of his films. No clutter about them either. The program is over in just ninety minutes. What have we seen?

> Boy maybe eighteen
> bent over snapshots while his
> cat licks itself clean.

> Naked girl, leading
> suitors a merry chase: she'll
> leave them stripped, bleeding—

this last to courtly music by Rameau. And finally

a dead youth. The shore's
gray, smooth, chill curve. His flesh a
single fly explores.

Strategies.

HALFWAY around the globe from Paul the worst keeps dawning on us. We try to conjure him up as he was only last winter: hair silvered early, the trustful, inquisitive, near-sighted face, the laugh one went to such lengths to hear. His book was practically done, he'd quit biting his nails. Well, now he knows, as do we; and the date line, like a great plateglass revolving door, or the next six-foot wave in an epic poem, comes flashing up to face the music. I need a form of conscious evasion, that at best permits odd moments when the subject

> looking elsewhere strays
> into a local muse's
> number-benumbed gaze

—fixed there, ticking off syllables, until she blinks and the wave breaks. Coming to, once again drenched, a fugitive, one is after all saner for the quarter-hour spent as a splotch of lichen upon that quaintest of stepping-stones.

Don't worry, I'm getting my share of fast food, TV news and tearjerkers, police running toward the explosion, our sickeningly clear connections to New York, a boîte called Wet Dream, the taximeter advancing, like history itself, by lifespans: 1880 to 1950 to 2020. Yet this automated Japan tends chiefly to mirror and amplify a thousandfold the writhing vocalist in my own red boîte, whom *I* want gagged, unplugged, shortcircuited. If every trip is an incarnation in miniature, let this be the one in which to arrange myself like flowers. Aim at composure like the target a Zen archer sees through shut eyes. Close my borders to foreign devils. Take for model a cone of snow with fire in its bowels.

Kyoto.

Daybreak. Brightest air
left brighter yet by hairline
cracks of gossamer.

TEMPLE pond—work of the mad priest who thought
he was a beaver? In the foreground roots scrawl their plea for
clemency upon a golden velvet scroll. *Granted,* breathe the
myriad starlets of moss, the dwarf maple's inch-wide asterisks.
The dead stump is tended as if it had never been more alive.
"To die without assurance of a cult was the supreme calamity."
(L. Hearn)

River Trip.

Short walk through fields to soft-drink stand where
boats wait—all aboard! Creak of rope oarlock. One man pulls
the single oar, another poles, a third steers, a fourth stands by
to relieve the first. High-up shrine, bamboo glade. Woodland
a cherry tree still in bloom punctuates like gunsmoke. Egret
flying upstream, neck cocked. Entering the (very gentle) rapids everyone gasps with pleasure. The little waves break back-
wards, nostalgia con moto, a drop of fresh water thrills the
cheek. And then? Woodland, bamboo glade, high-up shrine.
Years of this have tanned and shriveled the boatmen. For after
all, the truly exhilarating bits

> were few, far between
> —boulders goaded past, dumb beasts
> mantled in glass-green
>
> gush—and patently
> led where but to the landing,
> the bridge, the crowds. We

step ashore, in our clumsiness hoping not to spill these brief
impressions.

Afternoons at the Noh.

PLAYS of unself. Peel off the maiden pearl-diver to find her mother's ghost, the ghost to wake a dragon who, at the end of his dance, will attain Buddhahood. Masked as each of these in turn, the protagonist has the wattles and frame of

> a middle-aged man—
> but time, gender, self are laws
> waived by his gold fan.

Often depicted are the sufferings of poor people—woodcutters and fishermen, who nonetheless appear in uncommon finery. They've earned it. Each has entered the realm of legend and artifice, to become "a something else thereby." What glides before us is the ectoplasm of plot.

Enter today's ghost. Masked, longhaired and lacquer-bonneted, over his coral robe and white trousers he wears a coat of stiff apple-green gauze threaded with golden mazes. In life he was the warrior prince Tsunemasa. Before long, stirred by a votive lute *we* don't hear, he will relive moonlight, storm and battle, and withdraw, having danced himself to peace. At present the stage picture is static, a problem in chess. The eight-pawn chorus is chanting in antiphon with Tsunemasa— a droning, fluctuating,

> slowly-swelling hymn:
> the god's fingertip circling
> one deep vessel's rim

after another, until all the voices are attuned.

The drummer with a thimbled fingertap neat as a pool shot cuts short his vocalise at once resumed: a guttural growl that ends falsetto, hollow pearl balanced upon a jet of water,

full moon kept at bay
above Death Valley by the
wolf-pack roundelay.

The music has no purpose, Professor Shimura insists, but to
mark time for the actors. Blindfolded by their masks, ori-
ented, if at all, by the peripheral pine tree or stage pillar, they
need whatever help they can get. (Then why *this* music, so
animal, so ghostly?)

Feet in white socks explore the stage like palms of a blind
man. When they stamp it is apt to be without impact, the
dancer having levitated unawares. Hands are held relaxed but
gravely furled. Middle knuckles aligned with thumb unbent
compose half a right angle. Into the hollow that results may be
set a fan or willow-branch. Nothing easier than to withdraw it.
Hands like these will never clench or cling or stupidly dangle
or helplessly be wrung. They are princes to be served and de-
fended with one's life. My own hand as I write, wielding this
punctilious lance of blue, belongs to a lower caste.

A story Paul heard from an old Surrealist in Pau:
The Emperor's boyhood friend was convicted of treason and
sentenced to death by decapitation. In honor of their former
intimacy, the Emperor ordered the execution before dawn,
after a banquet for his friend at which the Court dancers would
appear. That legendary troupe could perform anything: the
Spider Web, A Storm at Sea, the Nuptials of the Phoenix. On
this occasion they outdid themselves. Yet well before the stars
had set, the doomed man turned to his host: "The Son of
Heaven has shown unmerited consideration, but really, can't
we call it a night and conclude our business without further
ado?" The Emperor raised his eyebrows: "My poor friend," he
smiled, "haven't you understood? Your head was cut off an
hour ago."

Oki Islands, a week later, after dinner. The maid, miming anticipation, slides open doors onto a little scrim of pine trees flat and black against the dazzle.

> Waves whisper. Tonight
> the netmender's deaf son reads
> their lips by moonlight,

but the real drama is due to go on elsewhere. Already owls and crickets are studying the program in silence. Long minutes pass. Imperceptibly the moon's ripeness comes to us bruised by some imminent "shadow of a thought." A dark thought that fills the psyche, leaving a bare brilliant cuticle, then nothing, a sucked breath, a pall. The stars crowd forward, like wizards round a sickbed. The goddess has donned her

> brownest mask: malign
> pomegranate, carbon-stifled
> ember—muss es sein?

Not this time. Watch:
Minim by scruple the high renaissance . . .
Celestial recovery. Doctors amazed. Altogether grander and more mysterious than anything at the Noh, yet from what lesser theater did we absorb the patience and piety needed to bring the moonlight back?

Dozen.

CIRCLING the island. Fantastic volcanic forms, dragon-coil outcrops nostril-deep in clear water—or so it might have been. But this stormy noon we're alone in the boat, screens of mist enfold the heights, and the famous drowned savannas, green-gold or violet-pink in travel posters, come through as dim, splitsecond exposures during which

> one seaweed fan waves
> at another just under
> from above the waves.

Kyogen Interlude: At the Bank.

I T is by now clear that the poor flushed clerk—a trainee's badge on his lapel—knows nothing. Fifty minutes have passed, our travelers checks are still being processed, and we have missed our train to Koyasan.

Donald (*at the counter, smiling gleefully*): Excuse me, would you kindly ask your supervisor to step this way?

Clerk (*in sudden English*): No. Please, he. Today not here.

Donald (*still in Japanese*): Nonsense. It's Monday morning. Everyone's here.

Clerk: I. No. He.

Donald: Because if you do not fetch him I shall be obliged to go and ask for him myself.

The clerk pales and vanishes, returning accompanied by an older man in neat shirtsleeves—the supervisor—who asks how he can be of service.

Donald: Good morning. My name is R___. I am a writer and journalist living in Tokyo. Allow me to give you my card.

Manners require that a card be studied by its recipient with every show of genuine interest. The supervisor beautifully clears this first hurdle. Donald resumes. During his tirade his listener's breathing quickens, his eyes glitter. He and the red-faced clerk, side by side, are contemplating the abyss to whose brink we've led them. The younger man, slightly bent, hands clasped at his crotch, has braced himself like one about to be flogged.

Donald: . . . and furthermore I shall speak of this on my return to Tokyo.

Supervisor (*face carefully averted from the culprit*): See here, you've been trained. Are you still incapable of a simple transaction? Then find someone in the office to take over. This is Osaka, not your village. I hold you responsible for a great rudeness to these distinguished guests.

To every phrase the clerk winces assent. Trays of clean money appear, which having pocketed we take our leave.

Supervisor *(bowing us to the door):* There is no apology for such a mortifying affair.

Donald: Please, it is of no consequence. I mentioned it only to spare your bank any future embarrassment.

JM *(on the eventual slower train):* Will you really make a fuss in Tokyo?

Donald: Goodness, no. What do you take me for?

Eleanor *(hearing it told months later):* Yes, that's what Mother used to call The Scene. As a child I watched her make it all over the world. You begin by saying you're an intellectual. It strikes the fear of God into them, I can't think why. Not here in America, of course, but anywhere else—! How do you think I got on that air-conditioned bus in Peru? How do you think I got out of East Berlin that ghastly Christmas? I told them I was a writer and journalist. I made The Scene.

DJ *(amused in spite of himself):* That story wasn't nice. Even bank clerks have to live.

Eleanor: Darling boy, nobody has to live. It's what I came away from Paul's service thinking. Nobody has to live.

Sanctum.

ANOTHER proscenium. At its threshold we sit on our heels, the only audience. Pure bell notes, rosaries rattled like dice before the throw. Some young priests—the same who received us yesterday, showed us to our rooms, served our meal, woke us in time for these matins—surround a candlelit bower of bliss. The abbot briskly enters, takes his place, and leads them in deep, monotonous chant. His well-fed back is to us. He faces a small gold pagoda flanked by big gold lotus trees overhung by tinkling pendants of gold. Do such arrangements please a blackened image deep within? To us they look like Odette's first drawing room (before Swann takes charge of her taste) lit up for a party, or the Maison Dorée he imagines as the scene of her infidelities. Still, when the abbot turns, and with a gesture invites us to place incense upon the brazier already full of warm, fragrant ash, someone—myself perhaps—tries vainly

> to hold back a queer
> sob. Inhaling the holy
> smoke, praying for dear

life—

Bunraku.

THE very river has stopped during Koganosuke's dialogue with his father. All at once—heavens!—the young man takes up a sword and plunges it into his vitals. There is no blood. He cannot die. The act will end with his convulsive efforts to. Meanwhile the rapids that divide him from his beloved begin to flow again—blue-and-white cardboard waves jiggled up and down—so that the lacquer box containing her head may be floated across to where he quakes, upheld by three mortals in black.

> (Into the Sound, Paul,
> we'd empty your own box, just
> as black, just as small.)

The lovers neither spoke nor acted—how could they? Their words came from the *joruri*, or reciter, who shares with the samisen player a dais at the edge of the stage. Upon taking his place the *joruri* performs an obeisance, lifting the text reverently to his brow. It is a specialized art—what art is not?—and he glories in it. He has mastered Koganosuke's noble accents, the heroine's mewing, and the evil warlord's belly-laugh which goes on for minutes and brings down the house. To function properly each puppet requires three manipulators. These, with the *joruri*, are the flesh and blood of this National Theater, and come to stand for—stand *in* for—the overruling passions, the social or genetic imperatives, that propel a given character. Seldom do we the living, for that matter, feel more "ourselves" than when spoken through, or motivated, by "invisible" forces such as these. It is especially true if, like a puppet overcome by woe, we also appear to be struggling free of them. (Lesser personages make do with two manipulators, or only one.)

> ". . . wonderful today . . . !"
> you yawned that night. It moved me:
> words began to play

like a fountain deep
in gloom. Did love reach out your
arm then? Sorrow? Sleep?

Geiger Counter

Pictures on a wall:
a *View of Fuji* challenged
by *The Dying Gaul.*

Syringe in bloom. Bud
drawn up through a stainless stem—
O perilous blood!

Tests, cultures . . . Weeks from
one to the next. That outer
rim of the maelstrom

hardly moved. Its core
at nightmare speed churned onward,
a devolving roar:

Awake—who? why here?
what room was this?—till habit
shaded the lit fear.

"YOU'RE not dying! You've been reading too much
Proust, that's all! I could be dying too—have you thought of
that, JM?—except that I don't happen to be sick, and neither
do you. What we *are* suffering are sympathetic aches and
pains. Guilt, if you like, over staying alive. Four friends have
died since December, now Paul's back at the Clinic. You were
right,"—the dying *Paul,* what else?—"we should have
scrapped the trip as soon as we heard. But God! even if you
and I *were* on the way out, wouldn't we still fight to live a bit
first, fully and joyously?"

Such good sense. I want to bow, touch my forehead to the
straw mat. Instead: "Fight? Like this morning? We can live *or*
die without another of those, thank you." Mutual glares.

The prevailing light in this "Hiroshima" of trivial symptoms and empty forebodings is neither sunrise nor moonglow but rays that promptly undo whatever enters their path. They strip the garden to clawed sand. They whip the modern hotel room back into fatal shape: the proportions and elisions of centuries. In their haste to photograph Truth they eat through a blue-and-white cotton robe, barely pausing to burn its pattern onto the body shocked alert:

> "What's the story, Doc?"
> —dark, cloud-chambered negatives
> held to the light. Knock,

knock. Not dinnertime already? Donald, making his ghoul face, joins us for another feast less of real food than of artfully balanced hues and textures. "I'm sick," sighs the sunburnt maid who serves it, and whose kimono we think to please her by admiring, "sick of wrapping myself up like a dummy day after day." Has the radiation affected her, too? And what *about* this morning's blinding outburst?

Another Cemetery.

W E pass it on our descent from the temple. The gravestones are vertically incised with the deceased's new name, the name assumed after death. Only by knowing it can a friend or kinsman hope to locate one's tomb among so many others. They all—untapering stone shafts on broad plinths— look exactly like scale models for skyscrapers in the 1930s. Intelligent intervals separate them. Light and air will have been of prime importance to whoever planned this "city of to-morrow," its little malls and avenues half-lost in foliage, and took care to place its ugly realities out of sight. In today's cold drizzle we feel he was not wholly successful. Oh for a glowing hearth to come home to!—as another name sputters, a

> last flickering shift
> of flame flutters off. The log's
> charred forked shape is left.

(Sold up at the temple, distant cousin to both the gravestone and the "Plant-Tab" stuck in a flowerpot to release nutrients over weeks to come: the incense stick. This, brittle, narrow slab of dark green, set upright in the burner's ash-heap and lit, will also turn to ash. But in the process, as it whitens, a hith-erto unseen character appears, below it a second, slowly a third, each traced by the finest penpoint of incandescence. They cool the way ink dries. Once complete and legible, their pious formula can be scattered by a touch. Any fragrance meanwhile eludes me. Have I caught cold?)

In the Shop.

Out came the most fabulous kimono of all: dark, dark purple traversed by a winding, starry path. To what function, dear heart, could it possibly be worn by the likes of—

Hush. Give me your hand. Our trip has ended, our quarrel was made up. Why couldn't the rest be?

Dyeing. A homophone deepens the trope. Surrendering to Earth's colors, shall we not *be* Earth before we know it? Venerated therefore is the skill which, prior to immersion, inflicts upon a sacrificial length of crêpe de Chine certain intricate knottings no hue can touch. So that one fine day, painstakingly unbound, this terminal gooseflesh, the fable's whole eccentric

> star-puckered moral—
> white, never-to-blossom buds
> of the mountain laurel—

may be read as having emerged triumphant from the vats of night.

V

WALKS IN ROME

Little has changed. Of the buildings—tufted clay,
Like tennis courts upended—
Some to this day won't see a dentist.
Others, robed in light green, head to toe,
For on-the-spot surgery, won't see us.
The senior ones, as when the family doctor
Closing the consultation
Doffs his white jacket for a chat or chess game,
Have stripped to the gruff brick. Those latterday
Sutures of iron hint
At the dramatically rose-lit
Martyrdom within, while the protruding giant
Veined foot reminds the patient that it's all
A dream. Only a dream?
If so, one we can walk the whole night through,

Arm in arm, like lovers in a story.
(Or can we?—"Amore! Tesoro!"—OK, wise guy!
—As the unerring Vespa whipping by
Takes the word out of my mouth. Amore.)

And walk whole days through rusty, falling leaves
Above the river racing still.
It will never grow up, suffer the frugal houseboat,
The coal barge. Better one dragonfly
Scull hovering in place. Better an Angel's
Bird-of-prey shadow rippling
Down from his ramparts. Yet once we descend, you and I,
To the cobbled embankment, push through gangling weeds,
Acne of burrs, to the brink,
Tiber, as usual instinctively
Sweeping itself from view, wakes the reflection:
It knows how to live!—
Current so debonair, so vital, why
Personified in sculpture with an urn,
Bearded, funereal, recumbent?
As I begin to follow, my eyes burn

Walks in Rome

The bridge of years. I feel in my old bones
A young man's dread. His longing. To be cast
Upon the waters! Pleasure sauntering past
Looked back? He sank into these very stones

Now gilt with mist. Our trattoria empties.
Tall in the Ptolemaic night
Houses red wine unsteadies reminisce.
That was Umberto's window, this was mine.
That bijou penthouse? Josie
Lived there one winter. Rome is a time exposure.
From his black square Orion cuts degrees
Of adamant whereby the here-below
Church, palace, obelisk,
Boarded-up flower stall, *our* square, all grow
Solider, and with each whispered nothing,
Each fading cry, more "eternal,"
While the cars, the people—? Just a human smear
About the Bocca della Verità,
Then eerie, disembodied shots of light
Down a late artery. It develops
We've all along had somewhere else to go.

The friends of 1986 are Swiss.
Italian men, discos and Art Deco,
Fashion and Hollywood are what they know.
Gowns by Hadrian?—Here Antinous,

Everyone's favorite,
Enters the strobe-lit crypt in shock. Despite
The warm blue honey of his glances,
Golden hair and mornings at the gym,
He didn't get the part. *Too old,* said Truth,
Adding lines left and right:
My monumental chronicles drag on.
Life glitters once, an epigram, and—gone.
Time now to walk him home?
Anything but! Tour instead the sedated

Fountains of 4 a.m.? Half awake, offer
Our balcony's coming attractions?—
Bells wrangling, cappucino,
Charioteers of the marble Typewriter
Driving their team through bare sky, winged with flame;
Dew-glazed below, the neighborhood Franciscans'
Kitchen garden. Not his scene,
He smiles, blowing a kiss

And gliding off—our cavalier of stealth
Turning the nearest corner, lest we see him
Make for that blackest mass, the Colosseum,
Whose faithful have stayed up to drink his health.

Chessboards, buried one beneath the other,
How slow, how fierce the contests
That foundered each. . . . Yet a young pawn I spent
Two years as (if time kept
So to oneself was spendable) blinks round him,
Dazed. For the opponent—thank you, Angel?—
Whose "men" and "moves" he parried is no more.
Problem solved? If not, its weight commuted
To levels underfoot
Where now-classic solutions rest in pieces
Hard to pry loose. The new subway
Performed a bypass through them, but how slowly:
Checked by the bone bishop of a cell
Fetid with faith, or queen's encaustic chamber
Blossoming deep in the hive—
Work held up (two more years? porca Madonna!)
For fear that, looked too closely at by day,
The nectarine would peel,
And mote by mote the cupid fly away.

Malaise of airports. Even this morning's King
Charles spaniel knew his hour on Earth was done;
Kenneled as baggage, howled. I wrote: Dear One,
My westbound high noon is your evening,

You've climbed—you promised—to a certain sunny
Outlook above trees in shade.
Overhead, the choral molecules
Will have already formed, their least electron
Blackly twinkling. Starlings, little stars.
On a vast slide you'll study
The life in one gold drop of heaven's blood—
Rapidly overlapping rival circuses,
Like animated ink
Drawings by Mirò—till a motif
Out of the ancient city comes alive:
Gladiators' nets, the mortal
Fling and pounce reborn, over the ages,
As play. The victims too
React good-humoredly. They are big trees now,
Used in their noble calling,
Night after night, to dreams of suffocation,
Chattering burdens—*nothing* (Truth to tell)
The sunrise won't dispel.
Remember that. Who loves you? Write. Keep well.

GRAFFITO

Deep in weeds, on a smooth chunk of stone
Fallen from the cornice of the church
(Originally a temple to Fortuna),
Appears this forearm neatly drawn in black,
Wearing, lest we misunderstand,
Like a tattoo the cross-within-a-circle
Of the majority—Christian Democrat.

Arms and the man. This arm ends in a hand
Which grasps a neatly, elegantly drawn
Cock—erect and spurting tiny stars—
And balls. One sports . . . a swastika?
Yes, and its twin, if you please, a hammer-and-sickle!
The tiny stars, seen close, are stars of David.
Now what are we supposed to make of that?

Wink from Lorenzo, pout from Mrs. Pratt.
Hold on, I want to photograph this latest
Fountain of Rome, whose twinkling gist
Gusts my way from an age when isms were largely
Come-ons for the priapic satirist,
And any young guy with a pencil felt
He held the fate of nations in his fist.

GRACE

All this is very tiring,"
The old, old woman sighed:
"Another railroad station . . ."
Which one today? In her time
She'd traveled, seen the world
Forming its vast impression,
The Gare des Invalides,
The Termini in Rome—
A vault of groans and grime,
Triumphant engineering
Each dawn shone sicklier through.
Now clocks were striking, she'd be going home

—But with an artful smile
Lay back in her hospital bed:
"This one I designed
Myself, though. Glassed-in wings
Overlook the Nile,
So you can lie back and read
Or sleep if at the last
Moment you decide
To take tomorrow's train instead."

The girders of the mind
Were twisting. Pane by pane
Her spattered sense of things
All autumn had been caving
Inward to this bead
Full of its own dry light,
With just room for a river,
One plume of smoke, one bird . . .
Tinier locomotives
Each afternoon kept leaving
Without her for the Valley of the Kings.
Each night's rain fell unheard.

ICECAP

Yes, melting changes
  the whole picture. That
once young republic tassled
sea to sea with golden wit
   has tattered to a
   wrack of towns, bubble
domes unpricked on the lagoon's
fogged mirror. Losses and debts
   are equally, now,
   past calculation,
resources (but for the odd
oil rig or artisan or
   lone—ah my dearest—
   body ardently
asleep beneath a sunset-
rippled vault of stucco) nil.
   Still, the shift from world
   power to tourist
mecca goes unmourned. People
appear relieved of the real
   embarrassment the
landscape had become
in those late decades. Dead roads
and deconsecrated malls,
   moth-eaten orchards
   far North, deep crops left
rotting on the Plains gave out
how the collective psyche
   shrugged off its future
   and despised its roots,
bent upon pleasures merely
of the here and now. Wherefore
   toward those gossamer
   centers all night long
causeways whip and barges throb.
By air—thanks to this morning's

Icecap

cold front, sharp enough,
following weeks of
doggedly adolescent
weather, to wake reflection
even in shallows—
breeding grounds, rather,
for a small scavenger crab,
the local delicacy—
by air on the hour
arrive not only
the groups but: bonsai birches,
Brie, vaccines and lenses, out-
of-date ensembles
in tomorrow's shades,
correction fluid Mister
Magoo (the draftsman's cat) can,
deft paw dipped, spatter
across the blueprint;
neatest of all, a fine-gauge
20-carat wire, from which
our morose goldsmith
on the Bridge of Smiles
has already fashioned this
shimmering, cereal wand.
Wear it, Milady,
in your frosted hair.

CORNWALL

Wind clear and heavy as a paperweight,
Lead crystal in which flowerets are set,

Sunburst-, trumpet-, bell-, spire-, star-shaped choirs
That faintly shudder at the names we pluck

Out of the handbook: rupturewort, wild carrot,
Thrift, self-heal, and—recognized too late

From fairy tales—the nettle, freckling fiery
White your windburned knuckles. Over this whole

Knee-deep enchanted cliff-top forest spreads
Iseult's Hair (shall we call it?), fine and coppery

Proof against wind, as if in wind outstreaming.
The sea, too, has grown eerily placid. Seams

Ennoble features like a dreaming titan's,
Taken for shelter. Rarely are outsiders

Shown these cramped conditions. But now under lichened
Brows flash sudden mica-chip embrasures,

Into the living vein the raindrop snuggles,
Some least quartz kernel, grit of the homestretch,

Grows lucid. We're already there, and learning
Symmetry, obliqueness, breadth of beam,

Weight of quilt, and have glimpsed beyond mote and carat
Suspended in the weak, lead-crystal light

That tiny medicine chest where the two vials—
Put away long ago for us—are gleaming:

One of brown glass with skull-and-crossbones label,
The other frosted, near empty, exhaling Joy.

LOSING THE MARBLES

for John Malcolm Brinnin

I
Morning spent looking for my calendar—
Ten whole months mislaid, name and address,
A groaning board swept clean . . .
And what were we talking about at lunch? Another
Marble gone. These latter years, Charmides,
Will see the mind eroded featureless.

Ah. We'd been imagining our "heaven"'s.
Mine was to be an acrobat in Athens
Back when the Parthenon—
Its looted nymphs and warriors pristine
By early light or noon light—dwelt
Upon the city like a philosopher,
Who now—well, you have seen.

Here in the gathering dusk one could no doubt
"Rage against the dying of the light."
But really—rage? (So like the Athens press,
Breathing fire to get the marbles back.)
These dreamy blinkings-out
Strike me as grace, if I may say so,
Capital punishment,
Yes, but of utmost clemency at work,
Whereby the human stuff, ready or not,
Tumbles, one last drum-roll, into thyme,
Out of time, with just the fossil quirk
At heart to prove—hold on, don't tell me . . . What?

2

Driving its silver car into the room,
The storm mapped a new country's dry and wet—
Oblivion's ink-blue rivulet.
Mascara running, worksheet to worksheet
Clings underfoot, exchanging the wrong words.
The right ones, we can only trust will somehow
Return to the tongue's tip,
Weary particular and straying theme,
Invigorated by their dip.

Invigorated! Gasping, shivering
Under our rough towels, never did they dream—!
Whom mouth-to-mouth resuscitation by
Even your *Golden Treasury* won't save,
They feel their claim
On *us* expiring: starved to macron, breve,
Those fleshless ribs, a beggar's frame . . .
From the brainstorm to this was one far cry.

Long work of knowing and hard play of wit
Take their toll like any virus.
Old timers, cured, wade ankle-deep in sky.

Meanwhile, come evening, to sit
Feverishly restoring the papyrus.

3

    body, favorite
          gleaned,   at the
                    vital
            frenzy—

act and moonshaft, peaks
                    stiffening
            Unutter[able]
        the beloved's

                              slowly
          stained in the deep   fixed
               summer nights
        or,

            scornful   Ch[arm]ides,
                decrepitude
      Now, however, that
    figures also

                  body everywhere
           plunders and
what we cannot—from the hut's lintel
        flawed

                        white as
  sliced turnip   the field's brow.
      our old
    wanderings

home   palace, temple,
  having   of those blue foothills
    no further   clear
        fancy[.]

4

Seven ages make a crazy quilt
Out of the famous web. Yet should milk spilt
(As when in Rhetoric one's paragraph
Was passed around and each time cut in half,
From eighty words to forty, twenty, ten,
Before imploding in a puff of Zen)
White out the sense and mutilate the phrase,
My text is Mind no less than Mallarmé's.
My illustration? The Cézanne oil sketch
Whose tracts of raw, uncharted canvas fetch
As much per square inch as the fruit our cloyed
Taste prizes for its bearing on the void.
Besides, Art furnishes a counterfeit
Heaven wherein ideas escape the fate
Their loyal adherents—brainwashed, so to speak,
By acid rain—more diatribes in Greek—
Conspicuously don't. We diehard few
Embark for London on the QE2.
Here mornings can be spent considering ours
Of long ago, removed and mute, like stars
(*Un*like vociferous Melina, once
A star herself, now Minister of Stunts).
Removed a further stage, viewed from this high wire
Between the elegiac and the haywire,
They even so raise questions. Does the will-
To-structural-elaboration still
Flute up, from shifting dregs of would-be rock,
Glints of a future colonnade and frieze?
Do higher brows unknit within the block,
And eyes whose Phidias and Pericles
Are eons hence make out through crystal skeins
Wind-loosened tresses and the twitch of reins?
Ah, not for long will marble school the blood
Against the warbling sirens of the flood.

87

Losing the Marbles

All stone once dressed asks to be worn. The foam-
Pale seaside temple, like a palindrome,
Had quietly laid its plans for stealing back.
What are the Seven Wonders now? A pile
Of wave-washed pebbles. Topless women smile,
Picking the smoothest, rose-flawed white or black,
Which taste of sunlight on moon-rusted swords,
To use as men upon their checkerboards.

5
The body, favorite trope of our youthful poets . . .
    With it they gleaned, as at the sibyl's tripod,
        insight too prompt and vital for words.
            Her sleepless frenzy—

cataract and moonshaft, peaks of sheer fire at dawn,
    dung-dusted violets, the stiffening dew—
        said it best. Unutterable too
            was the beloved's

save through the index of refraction a fair, slowly
    turned head sustained in the deep look that fixed him.
        From then on veining summer nights with
            flickering ichor,

he had joined an elite scornful—as were, Charmides,
    your first, chiseled verses—of decrepitude
        in any form. Now, however, that
            their figures also

begin to slip the mind—while the body everywhere
    with peasant shrewdness plunders and puts to use
        what we cannot—from the hut's lintel
            gleams one flawed image;

another, cast up by frost or earthquake, shines white as
    sliced turnip from a furrow on the field's brow.
        Humbly our old poets knew to make
            wanderings into

homecomings of a sort—harbor, palace, temple, all
    having been quarried out of those blue foothills
        no further off, these last clear autumn
            days, than infancy.

6
Who gazed into the wrack till
Inspiration glowed,
Deducing from one dactyl
The handmaiden, the ode?

Or when aphasia skewered
The world upon a word,
Who was the friend, the steward,
Who bent his head, inferred

Then filled the sorry spaces
With pattern and intent,
A syntax of lit faces
From the impediment?

                    No matter, these belated
Few at least are back. And thanks
To their little adventure, never so
Brimming with jokes and schemes,
Fussed over, fêted
By all but their fellow saltimbanques—
Though, truth to tell,
Who by now doesn't flip
Hourly from someone's upper story
("That writer . . . no, on shipboard . . . wait . . . Charmides?")
And come to, clinging to the net?
And yet, and yet
Here in the afterglow
It almost seems
Death has forgotten us
—As the old lady said to Fontenelle.
                    And he,
A cautionary finger to his lip:
"Shh!"

7
After the endless jokes, this balmy winter
Around the pool, about the missing marbles,
What was more natural than for my birthday
To get—from the friend whose kiss that morning woke me—
A pregnantly clicking pouch of targets and strikers,
Aggies and rainbows, the opaque chalk-red ones,
Clear ones with DNA-like wisps inside,
Others like polar tempests vitrified . . .
These I've embedded at random in the deck-slats
Around the pool. (The pool!—compact, blue, dancing,
Lit-from-beneath oubliette.) By night their sparkle
Repeats the garden lights, or moon- or starlight,
Tinily underfoot, as though the very
Here and now were becoming a kind of heaven
To sit in, talking, largely mindless of
The risen, cloudy brilliances above.

INVESTITURE AT CECCONI'S

for David Kalstone

Caro, that dream (after the diagnosis)
found me losing patience outside the door of
"our" Venetian tailor. I wanted evening
clothes for the new year.

Then a bulb went on. The old woman, she who
stitches dawn to dusk in his back room, opened
one suspicious inch, all the while exclaiming
over the late hour—

Fabrics? patterns? those the proprietor must
show by day, not now—till a lightning insight
cracks her face wide: *Ma! the Signore's here to
try on his new robe!*

Robe? She nods me onward. The mirror triptych
summons three bent crones she diffracted into
back from no known space. They converge by magic,
arms full of moonlight.

Up my own arms glistening sleeves are drawn. Cool
silk in grave, white folds—Oriental mourning—
sheathes me, throat to ankles. I turn to face her,
uncomprehending.

Thank your friend, she cackles, *the Professore!*
Wonderstruck I sway, like a tree of tears. You—
miles away, sick, fearful—have yet arranged this
heartstopping present.

FAREWELL PERFORMANCE

for DK

Art. It cures affliction. As lights go down and
Maestro lifts his wand, the unfailing sea change
starts within us. Limber alembics once more
make of the common

lot a pure, brief gold. At the end our bravos
call them back, sweat-soldered and leotarded,
back, again back—anything not to face the
fact that it's over.

You are gone. You'd caught like a cold their airy
lust for essence. Now, in the furnace parched to
ten or twelve light handfuls, a mortal gravel
sifted through fingers,

coarse yet grayly glimmering sublimate of
palace days, Strauss, Sidney, the lover's plaintive
Can't we just be friends? which your breakfast phone call
clothed in amusement,

this is what we paddled a neighbor's dinghy
out to scatter—Peter who grasped the buoy,
I who held the box underwater, freeing
all it contained. Past

sunny, fluent soundings that gruel of selfhood
taking manlike shape for one last jeté on
ghostly—wait, ah!—point into darkness vanished.
High up, a gull's wings

clapped. The house lights (always supposing, caro,
Earth remains your house) at their brightest set the
scene for good: true colors, the sun-warm hand to
cover my wet one. . . .

Farewell Performance

Back they come. How you would have loved it. We in
turn have risen. Pity and terror done with,
programs furled, lips parted, we jostle forward
eager to hail them,

more, to join the troupe—will a friend enroll us
one fine day? Strange, though. For up close their magic
self-destructs. Pale, dripping, with downcast eyes they've
seen where it led you.

PROCESSIONAL

Think what the demotic droplet felt,
Translated by a polar wand to keen
Six-pointed Mandarin—
All singularity, its Welt-
Anschauung of a hitherto untold
Flakiness, gemlike, nevermore to melt!

But melt it would, and—look—become
Now birdglance, now the gingko leaf's fanlight,
To that same tune whereby immensely old
Slabs of dogma and opprobrium,
Exchanging ions under pressure, bred
A spar of burnt-black anchorite,

Or in three lucky strokes of word golf LEAD
Once again turns (LOAD, GOAD) to GOLD.

A NOTE ABOUT THE AUTHOR

James Merrill was born in New York City and now lives in Stonington, Connecticut. He is the author of ten earlier books of poems, which have won him two National Book Awards (for *Nights and Days* and *Mirabell*), the Bollingen Prize in Poetry (for *Braving the Elements*) and the Pulitzer Prize (for *Divine Comedies*). *From the First Nine: Poems* 1946–1976, a selection from his first nine books, appeared in 1982 with a companion volume, *The Changing Light at Sandover*, which included the long narrative poem begun with "The Book of Ephraim" (from *Divine Comedies*), plus *Mirabell: Books of Number* and *Scripts for the Pageant* in their entirety. The latter received the Book Critics Circle Award in poetry for 1983. *Late Settings* appeared in 1985. He has also written two novels, *The (Diblos) Notebook* (1965) and *The Seraglio* (1957, reissued in 1987) and two plays, *The Immortal Husband* (first produced in 1955 and published in *Playbook* the following year), and, in one act, *The Bait*, published in Artist's Theatre (1960). A book of essays, *Recitative*, appeared in 1986.

A NOTE ON THE TYPE

The text of this book was set in Plantin, a digitized version of a type face cut in 1913 by The Monotype Corporation, London. Though the face bears the name of the great Christopher Plantin, who in the latter part of the sixteenth century owned, in Antwerp, the largest printing and publishing firm in Europe, it is a rather free adaptation of designs by Claude Garamond (c. 1480–1561) made for that firm. With its strong, simple lines, Plantin is a no-nonsense face of exceptional legibility.

COMPOSITION BY GRAPHIC COMPOSITION, INC.,
ATHENS, GEORGIA

PRINTED AND BOUND BY HALLIDAY LITHOGRAPHERS,
WEST HANOVER, MASSACHUSETTS

DESIGNED BY HARRY FORD